GREET THE DAWN

SOUTH DAKOTA

STATE HISTORICAL SOCIETY PRESS

PIERRE

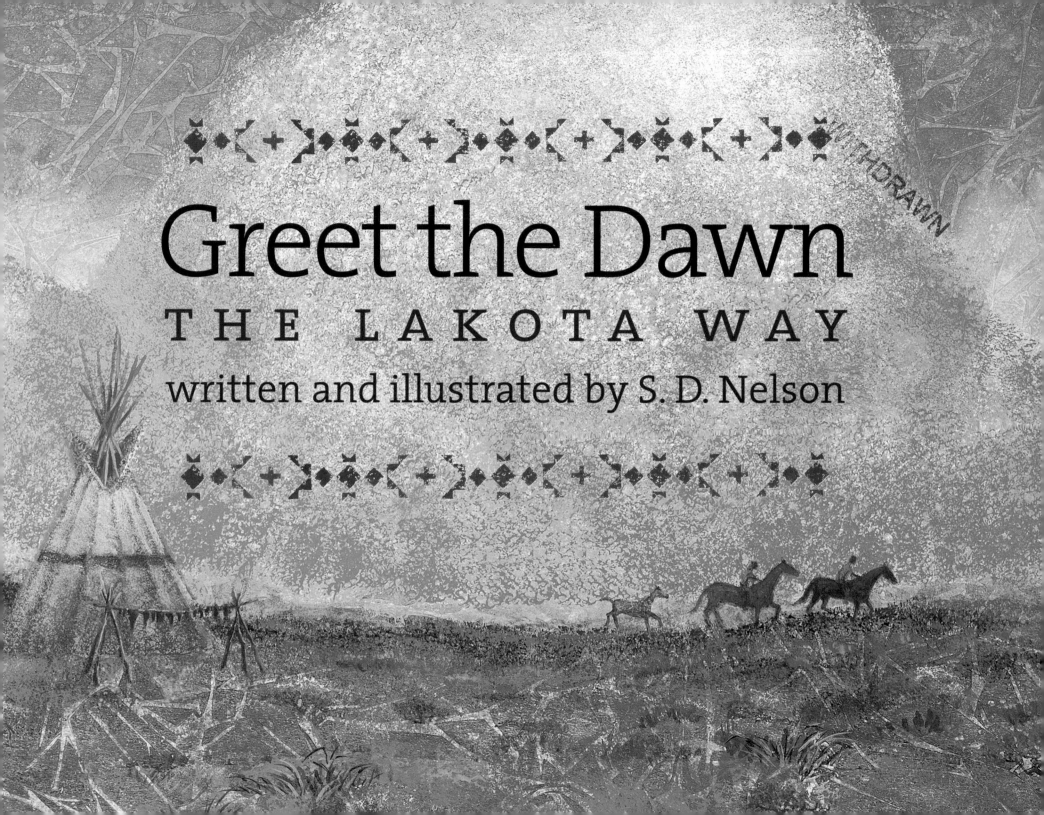

Greet the Dawn

THE LAKOTA WAY

written and illustrated by S. D. Nelson

© 2012 by the South Dakota State Historical Society Press

This publication was funded, in part, by the
Great Plains Education Foundation, Inc., Aberdeen, S.Dak.

Library of Congress Cataloging-in-Publication data
Nelson, S. D.
Greet the dawn : the Lakota way / written and illustrated by S. D. Nelson.
    p. cm.
ISBN 978-0-9845041-6-9
1. Teton philosophy—Juvenile literature.
2. Teton Indians—Religion—Juvenile literature. I. Title.
E99.T34N45 2012
978.004'9752—dc22
                                    2011013925
Printed in Canada

23   22   21   20   19   3   4   5   6   7

For Darcy, Wind-In-Her-Hair

Introduction

"Is not the sky a father and the earth a mother, and are not all living things
with feet or wings or roots their children?"— Black Elk (Oglala Lakota)

The Circle of Life is real for people who follow Lakota tradition. If you look and listen, you will see for yourself. Each day begins with the rising circle of Father Sun. He passes in an arc overhead. Sister Meadowlark knows the Lakota Way. She lays her little round eggs in the safe circle of her nest. Our Mother Earth is forever turning in a circle beneath us. At night, round Sister Moon circles above with the Star People. When we human beings hug the ones we love, we encircle them with our arms.

The Lakota Way offers a means of living in balance. Morning is a good time to begin the Lakota Way. Everything in the natural world has a spirit and is connected one to the other—the four-legged beings, the winged ones, the green growing things, the little creepy crawlies, and we two-legged beings. We call these beings our brothers and sisters. All beings journey with us during our lifetime. Even the moon, the stars, and the wind have a spirit. When we see rain clouds coming from the west, we call them Thunder Beings. We call the stars the Star People. Even the rocks upon the ground are called the Stone People.

The Lakotas were once a fierce warrior society. They were a renowned nomadic horse culture that hunted the vast herds of buffalo on the Great Plains of North America. They did not always live in harmony with their neighboring tribes, and they certainly struggled against the aggression of the United States military in the nineteenth century. Therein lies the paradox. There are two opposing forces that are fundamental to the world—order and chaos, good and evil.

There is a Great Spirit within all of creation. In the Lakota language, we call this power *Wakan Tanka*. More precisely, it means the Great Mystery; for everything in this universe is wondrous, perplexing at times, and beyond our comprehension. In truth, struggle and conflict are fundamental aspects of life on our planet. Beauty and goodness are also real.

In order to survive, we human beings must eat plants and consume animals—life must be taken so that we may live. With this awareness, we learn humility and find balance. Our lives need to be lived in a circle, not a square, nor a straight line.

If you look at our world, you will see the beauty of a flower petal and the danger of sharp teeth, for the way of the world can be both beautiful and cruel. Still, trouble and pain can be brought into balance with love and goodness. Living every day with a bitter heart offers no solution. It is better to greet the dawn with a smiling heart.

GREET THE DAWN

We greet the dawn with a smiling heart,

for all is beautiful at the beginning of a new day.

Father Sun gives warmth to Mother Earth.

Meadowlark sings her song as swallows fly above.

Our ancestors sang to the Great Spirit:

Le miye yelo

wanmayankiye yo.

Anpe wi kon miye yelo

wanmayanka yo.

Here I am

behold me.

I am the sun

behold me.

Dewdrops glisten as they cling to each green leaf.
They shimmer upon curving petals and dragonfly wings.

With a smiling heart, we feel the yellow glow

of Father Sun warm upon our faces.

Brother Eagle flies high with outstretched wings.

Our happy eyes see clouds dancing in the blue sky.

Our fathers sang:

Anpao

mawani nunwe

tato heya

mawani nunwe

anpao

mawani

kangi

hotonhan

mawani nunwe.

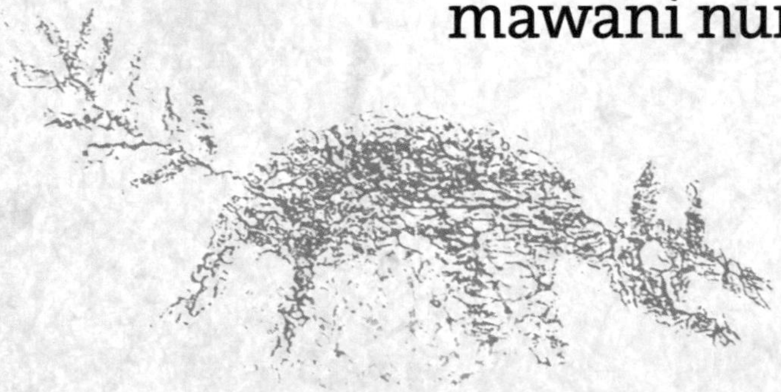

At dawn

may I roam

against the winds

may I roam

at dawn

may I roam

when the crow

is calling

may I roam.

Thank you for our four-legged brothers—

rabbit, deer, and buffalo.

Our Mother Earth gives us food and shelter.

She gives us everything we need.

Winds whisper, winds blow.

Storms come and storms go.

With happy ears, we listen

as raindrops p_itt_er- p_att_er.

We smell the sweet earth and

welcome the colors of Sister Rainbow.

Purple shadows lengthen.

All is beautiful with the passing of day.

Twinkling stars appear

above as fireflies flicker below.

We welcome Sister Moon with

a smiling heart.

Our ancestors sang to the Great Spirit:

Le miye yelo

wanmayanka yo

heya u welo.

Hanye wi kon he miye yelo

wanmayanka yo.

Here am I,

behold me,

it said as it rose.

I am the moon

behold me.

The song of crickets
and frogs fills the night.
Thank you for all the little
creepy-crawlies.

We two-legged beings

gather by firelight.

We give thanks for each day.

We celebrate this night.

With a smiling heart, our eyes close in sleep.

In our dreams, this day we will keep.

A Note about the Illustrations and Text

The illustrations for this book are a personal and contemporary interpretation of traditional Lakota imagery. My painting style has been directly influenced by American Indian pictographic images painted on buffalo hides and by ledger book drawings, in particular, for their bold use of line, shape, and color. Additionally, I have been inspired by the abstract geometric patterns found in Lakota quillwork and beadwork.

All of the acrylic paintings and pictographic drawings were done on heavy watercolor paper. I began each illustration by lightly texturing the paper with a mixture of gesso and modeling paste. I used brushes to lay down washes of color and sponges to create texture. In some areas I also used an atomizer to spray mists of blended color.

My mother taught me at an early age to see the world with both the curious eyes of a child and the wistful eyes of an old man. I learned that morning is the most beautiful time, for at dawn the world is born anew. It is the time when the winged-ones make their song, and the little green growing things are covered in precious dewdrops. At dawn, all is golden, all is beautiful.

The teachings of Black Elk, the Oglala Lakota holy man, have been most influential in my life. His words of wisdom are offered to all people in the wonderful book *Black Elk Speaks*, written by John Neihardt. The text of the Lakota-language songs in this book were recorded in Frances Densmore, *Teton Sioux Music* (1918). I am grateful to many other authors, such as Joseph Epes Brown, *The Sacred Pipe* (1953); Joseph M. Marshall III, *The Lakota Way* (2001); Royal B. Hassrick, *The Sioux* (1964); and Susan Power, *The Grass Dancer* (1994), for their influences in my life. Finally, I am especially grateful to the Lakota Sun Dancers who welcomed me into their Inipi ceremony (Lakota Sweat Lodge). From them I learned the old songs and the old ways. They taught me how to seek a vision and how to greet the dawn.